PEW!
The Stinky AND Legen-Dairy Gift
From COLONEL THOMAS S. MEACHAM

By **Cathy Stefanec Ogren**

and Illustrated by **Lesley Breen**

PUBLISHED by SLEEPING BEAR PRESS™

Colonel Thomas S. Meacham

of Sandy Creek, New York,
owned acres of fertile land,

workhorses,

beef cattle,

wooly sheep,
and . . .

150 dairy cows!

In late summer of 1835,
Thomas Meacham
wanted to give the
PRESIDENT OF THE UNITED STATES
a gift to show off the talents
of his farming community.

A slice of an idea grew
into a **huge idea,**
a **colossal idea . . .**

Cheese!

Not just any cheese, but a **mammoth** cheese,
a legendary gift made on Thomas Meacham's property.

A carpenter built a giant frame, hoop, and press.

Thomas Meacham's cows
filled pail after pail
with fresh, frothy milk.

The dairymen had to . . .
warm the milk,

add an ingredient to curdle it,

cut the curd into pieces,

separate it from the liquid whey,

break up the curd into smaller pieces,

press out the whey,

and crumble the curd.

Lined with a special cheesecloth,
the enormous hoop was ready for the final steps.

Over five days,
men filled the hoop
with the crumbled curds,

added salt,
and pressed out the
remaining whey.

But it wasn't big enough for
Thomas Meacham. He added more
crumbled curd until the wheel of
cheese reached ...

four feet in diameter,
two feet thick,
and weighed 1,400 pounds—
about as much as one of
Meacham's dairy cows.

Udderly amazing!

Ripe for delivery, the immense gift,
wrapped in patriotic pride,
was loaded onto a wagon.

Twenty-four teams of gray horses clip-clopped through town, pulling the cheese. Thomas Meacham invited area farmers to join the parade, which stretched for a mile.

A schooner in Port Ontario, New York,
waited for Thomas Meacham and his cheese to board.

People cheered,

music played,

cannons fired,

as they embarked on a
spectacular tour!

They sailed down canals,

lakes, and rivers.

OSWEGO

PORT ONTARIO

ERIE CANAL

SYRACUSE

TROY

ALBANY

Crowds of people admired the celebrated cargo as it reached each port.

NEW YORK CITY

PHILADELPHIA

DELAWARE RIVER

BALTIMORE

CHESAPEAKE BAY

WASHINGTON

January 15, 1836, was a day for celebration.

Thomas Meacham presented his cheese to the president of the
United States in the name of the "Governor and the people of
the State of New York and the Town of Sandy Creek."

Placed in the entrance hall of the White House, the enormous wheel stood there for over a year. The president carved out large chunks of cheese for his friends, but he still had more cheese than he could eat.

The hot, humid summer played mischief with the monster cheese, causing a *GHASTLY ODOR* to swirl around the White House.

One Washingtonian called it an *"EVIL-SMELLING HORROR."*

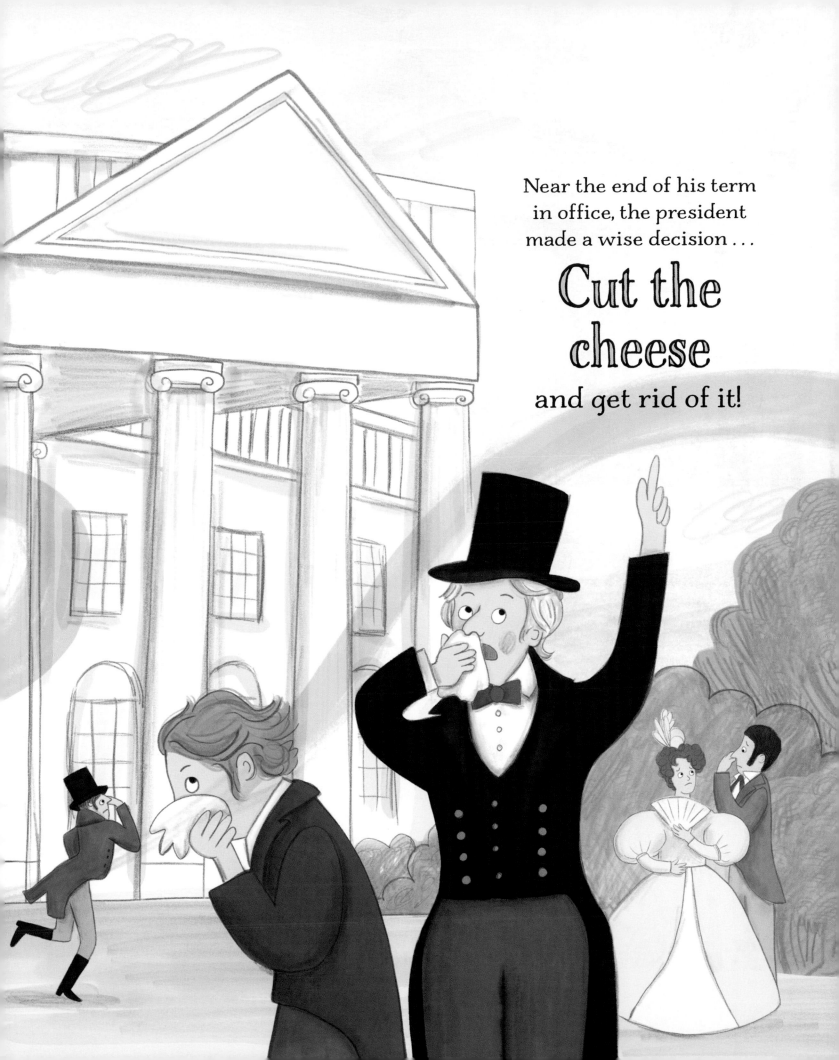

Near the end of his term in office, the president made a wise decision . . .

Cut the cheese

and get rid of it!

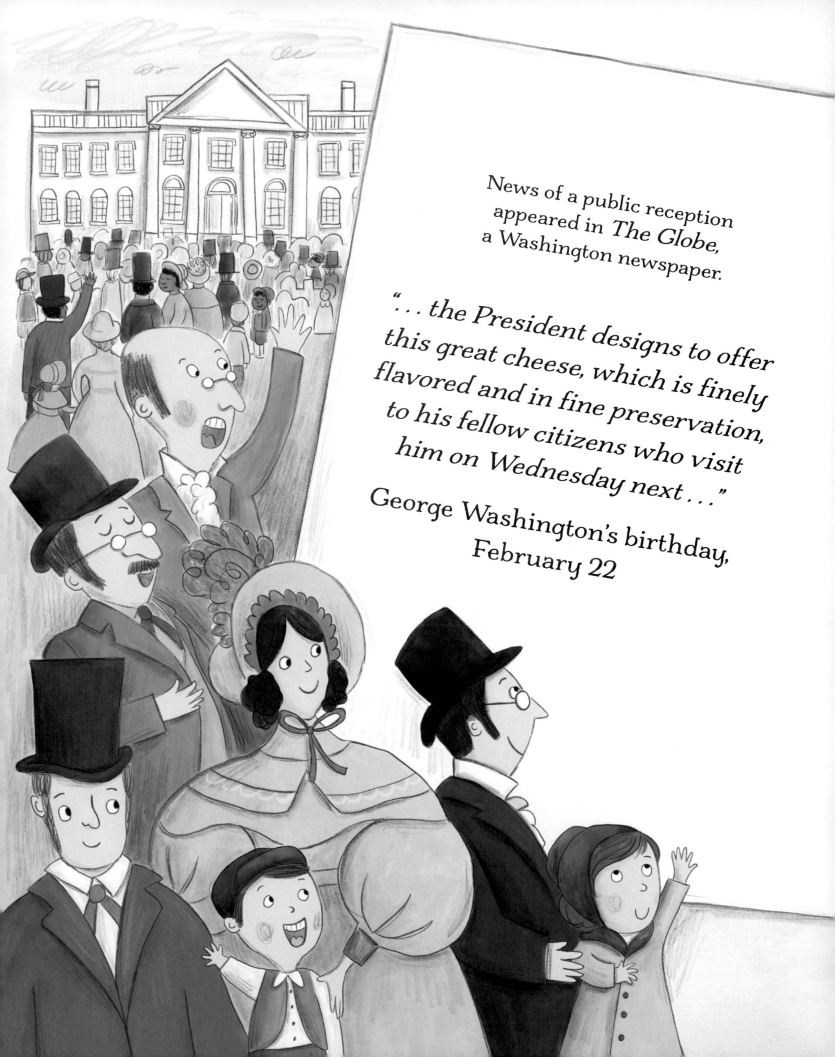

News of a public reception appeared in *The Globe*, a Washington newspaper.

"... the President designs to offer this great cheese, which is finely flavored and in fine preservation, to his fellow citizens who visit him on Wednesday next ..."

George Washington's birthday, February 22

Dignitaries,
diplomats,
government officials,

wealthy gentlemen,
fancy ladies,

ordinary citizens
headed to the White House
to eat cheese.

Ten thousand people showed up!

Crowds pushed and shoved through doors,
climbed through windows,
fought for chunks of cheese.

Cheese was on lips,

in mouths,

in hands,

in pockets.

Pieces littered the floor.
Boots ground them into carpets.
Drapes became napkins.

Two hours later, Thomas Meacham's mammoth cheese was gone.
All that was left was . . .

The incoming president had curtains removed,

carpets aired,

walls whitewashed and painted.

The foul odor of cheese lingered in the White House
for months until it finally disappeared.

The legen-dairy tale
of Colonel
Thomas S. Meacham's
big cheese ends here . . .

or does it?

Colonel Thomas S. Meacham served in the War of 1812. He owned the largest farm in Oswego County, New York, where he grew barley and wheat and sheared sheep for wool. The fertile soil of the small community of Sandy Creek was excellent for farming and planting.

A special ingredient called rennet was added to the warmed milk to make the milk curdle, or become solid. The watery liquid that remained after the milk curdled was called whey. The curd was cut into pieces, which released more whey, and then it was separated from the curds by pressing out the whey. It is unknown how Thomas Meacham accomplished the task of making the amount of curds needed to make his big cheese.

Thomas Meacham wrapped the circumference of the massive cheese with paper decorated with a bust of the president and drawings of the twenty-four states in the Union. It was inscribed: *The Union, it must be Preserved.*

The cheese traveled to Washington, D.C., beginning at Port Ontario, New York, and then to the town of Oswego. It was moved to a canal boat, and traveled on the Erie Canal to Syracuse. The cheese was displayed in Utica and Troy and then went on to Albany. Traveling down the Hudson River, it went to New York City. Another boat took the cheese down the Atlantic Coast to the Delaware River to Philadelphia, then to Baltimore by way of the Chesapeake Bay and on to Washington, D.C., on the Potomac River. The journey began on November 15, 1835, and ended on January 15, 1836.

For the president's final public party, the cheese was moved from the Entrance Hall, originally called the Vestibule, to the East Room. It was cut into hundreds and hundreds of pieces. Accounts differ as to which room was used for serving.

Along with Thomas Meacham's 1,400-pound prized cheese, several other 700-pound cheeses traveled with him. The smaller cheeses were given as gifts to dignitaries. After the president left the White House, his successor discovered a 700-pound cheese. He quickly got rid of it at a public auction for charity.

CHEESY FACTS

Cheese making was a way to preserve milk.

There are four basic ingredients used to make cheese. They are milk, salt, cultures (good bacteria), and rennet.

Salt is added to cheese to preserve it and prevent bad bacteria from growing.

In the past, hard cheeses were created from recipes when there was no refrigeration, which meant they could last for a long time without being kept cold.

Cheese was created by accident thousands of years ago when stomach linings of certain animals were used to store or transport milk. Enzymes in the stomach linings caused the milk to separate into solids and liquids—curds and whey.

It takes about ten pounds of milk to make one pound of cheese.

Some cheeses can help prevent tooth decay and protect tooth enamel.

Macaroni and cheese is one of the most popular dishes in the United States.

There are more than 2,000 varieties of cheese.

Stinky cheese and stinky feet may smell the same because they have the same bacterium.

SELECTED SOURCES

Archived Books

Johnson, Crisfield. *History of Oswego County, New York*. Philadelphia: L. H. Everts & Co., 1877, pages 377–378.

Johnson, Haynes. *The Working White House*. New York: Praeger Publishers, Inc., 1975, page 16.

Website

Winship, Kihm. "Cheese: From Sandy Creek to the White House." faithfulreaders.com/2012/11/28/cheese-from-sandy-creek-to-the-white-house/

Quotation Sources

Page 16: "Governor and the people of the State of New York and the Town of Sandy Creek." Sandy Creek, NY History Center. www.sandycreeknyhistory.com/historians-corner-5-27-16.htm

Page 18: "evil-smelling horror.": "Andrew Jackson's Big Block of Cheese." www.mentalfloss.com/article/27228/andrew-jacksons-big-block-cheese

Page 20: ". . . the President designs to offer this great cheese, which is finely flavored and in fine preservation, to his fellow citizens who visit him on Wednesday next": "Andrew Jackson's Big Block of Cheese: How a Quirky Gift Became a Political Legend." www.thoughtco.com/andrew-jacksons-big-block-of-cheese-1773414

Discrepancies of dates and places were found in the different sources used.

For my book-loving grandchildren, Emilia, Isabel, Malena, and Samuel.
May you always find joy in reading.
—C.S.O.

For Jeremy and "the boys"—Kiernan, Finn, and Dermot—Thanks for being you!
—L.B.

SLEEPING BEAR PRESS™

Sleeping Bear Press
2395 South Huron Parkway, Suite 200, Ann Arbor, MI 48104
www.sleepingbearpress.com © Sleeping Bear Press
Printed and bound in China.
10 9 8 7 6 5 4 3 2 1
Library of Congress Cataloging-in-Publication Data
Names: Ogren, Cathy Stefanec, author. | Breen, Lesley, illustrator.
Title: Pew! : the stinky and legen-dairy gift from Colonel Thomas S.
Meacham / written by Cathy Stefanec Ogren ; illustrated by Lesley Breen
Other titles: Stinky and legen-dairy gift from Colonel Thomas S. Meacham
Description: Ann Arbor, MI : Sleeping Bear Press, [2023] | Audience: Ages 6-10
| Summary: "In 1836, to call attention to his upstate New York
farming community, Colonel Thomas S. Meacham gives a mammoth wheel of
cheese to President Andrew Jackson. But after a year, the big cheese is
still around, causing a big stink in the White House"-- Provided by publisher.
Identifiers: LCCN 2022036753 | ISBN 9781534111936 (hardcover)
Subjects: LCSH: White House (Washington, D.C.)--Anecdotes--Juvenile
literature. | Jackson, Andrew, 1767-1845--Anecdotes--Juvenile
literature. | Presidents--United States--Anecdotes--Juvenile literature.
| Cheese--United States--Juvenile literature. | Meacham, Thomas S.,
1795-1847--Anecdotes--Juvenile literature.
Classification: LCC F204.W5 S733 2023 | DDC 975.3/02--dc23/eng/20220803
LC record available at https://lccn.loc.gov/2022036753